Java

Programming Basics for Absolute Beginners

Nathan Clark

Other Books in this Series

Computer Programming for Beginners

Fundamentals of Programming Terms and Concepts

a FREE Kindle Version with Paperback

JAVA

A Detailed Approach to Practical Coding

a FREE Kindle Version with Paperback

JAVA

Advanced Features and Programming Techniques

a FREE Kindle Version with Paperback

Table of Contents

Introduction

Welcome to the wonderful world of programming, the chapters contained in this book will give you a basic understanding of programming in Java. By its final chapter you will be able to create a complete program on your own, using Java.

This guide is aimed at newcomers to Java. If however you are completely new to programming, I recommend first reading our primer to programming. It covers all the concepts, terms, programming paradigms and coding techniques that a complete novice needs to know.

Computer Programming for Beginners
Fundamentals of Programming Terms and Concepts

An important aspect of this series, and your learning experience, is **learning by doing**. Practical examples are proven to be the best way to learn a programming language, which is why I have crammed as many examples into this guide as possible. I have tried to keep the core of the examples similar, so the only variable is the topic under discussion. This makes it easier to understand what we are implementing. As you progress through the chapters, remember to follow along with the examples and try them yourself.

In order to use the information contained in this book, you must have a computer that runs Windows, Macintosh, Linux, or UNIX operating system. You must know how to run a program, copy a file, create a folder, and navigate through menus. These are the only requirements for being able to program using Java.

Thank you for your interest in this versatile language and let's have some fun!

1. What is Java?

J ava is a programming language that is built by Sun Microsystems, which was later taken over by the Oracle Corporation. It is designed to run on any operating system that supports Java. This is what made the language so popular, because the developer just had to write the program once, and the program could then run on any operating system without the need for the programmer to change the code.

Most of the modern applications built around the world are made from the Java programming language. Most of the server side and business logic components of major applications are built on the Java programming language.

A sample Java program is shown below.

Example 1: The following program is used to showcase a simple Java program.

```
public class HelloWorld
{
    public static void main(String[] args) {
        System.out.println("Hello World!");
    }
}
```

During the entire course of this book you will learn how to write programs such as the one above, and also learn advanced concepts that will enable you to start writing complete application programs.

Some of the design goals for Java are mentioned below:

- The language is intended to be written once and have the ability to be run on any operating system.

- The language should provide support for numerous software engineering principles.

- The language is intended to be used in developing software components suitable for deployment in distributed environments.

- Portability is an important factor. This is why Java has the ability to run on Windows, Linux and the MacOS operating system.

- Support for internationalization is very important.

- Java is intended to be suitable for writing applications for both hosted and embedded systems.

Other design goals are discussed next.

1.1 Strong Type Checking

Java is a strong type language. Every variable that is defined needs to be attached to a data type. An example is shown below.

Example 2: The following program shows a strong typing example for the Java programming language.

```
public class HelloWorld
{
    public static void main(String[] args) {
        int i=5;
        System.out.println("The value of i is "+i);
    }
}
```

You don't need to understand the complete program for now, but let's just have a quick look at 2 lines of the code.

1) int i=5;

Here we are defining something known as a variable, which is used to hold a value. The value that can be stored depends on the data type. In this example we are saying that 'i' is of the type 'int' or Integer, which is a number data value.

2) System.out.println("The value of i is "+i)

Here we print the value of 'i' by means of the System.out.println statement. If we did not declare 'i' as an integer value, we would then get the below error if we had to compile the program.

HelloWorld.java:5: error: cannot find symbol

System.out.println("The value of i is "+i);

^

symbol: variable i

location: class HelloWorld

1 error

1.2 Array Bounds Checking

At runtime, Java will check whether the array has the required number of values defined. If one tries to access a value which is outside the bounds of the array, an exception will be thrown. An example is shown below.

Example 3: The following program is used to showcase array bounds checking.

```
public class HelloWorld
{
    public static void main(String[] args) {
        int[] array1 = new int[2];
        array1[0] = 1;
        array1[1] = 2;
        array1[2] = 3;
    }
}
```

You don't need to understand the complete program for now, but let's just have a quick look at the following lines of the code.

1) int[] array1 = new int[2];

Here we are declaring an array, which is a set of integer values. The value of '2' means that we can only store two values in the array.

2) array1[0] = 1;
   array1[1] = 2;
   array1[2] = 3;

With this code we can see that we are assigning 3 values to the array. When you run this program, you will get an error because the program will see that the array has gone out of its maximum allowable bounds of two. You will get the below error at runtime.

Exception in thread "main" java.lang.ArrayIndexOutOfBoundsException: 2 at HelloWorld.main(HelloWorld.java:8)

2. History of Java

The Java language was designed by James Gosling and first appeared on the scene in May of 1995. The programming language has gone through various releases, with the current version being version 8.

In the year 2006, Java had released the Java Virtual Machine. The Java Virtual Machine is used to run Java programs on the relevant operating systems, and was made available under free software/open-source distribution terms.

Below are the release date and the .net framework version for each Java version release.

Version	Release Date
JDK 1.0	January 23, 1996
JDK 1.1	February 19, 1997
J2SE 1.2	December 8, 1998
J2SE 1.3	May 8, 2000
J2SE 1.4	February 6, 2002
J2SE 5.0	September 30, 2004
Java SE 6	December 11, 2006
Java SE 7	July 28, 2011

Below we go into detail on the various versions of Java and the features which were introduced with each version.

JDK 1.1 - Support for the following:

- An extensive retooling of the AWT event model.

- Inner classes added to the language.

- JavaBeans.

- JDBC.

- RMI.

- Reflection, which supports Introspection only. No modification at runtime is possible.

- JIT (Just In Time) compiler on Microsoft Windows platforms, produced for JavaSoft by Symantec.

- Internationalization and Unicode support originating from Taligent.

J2SE 1.2 - Support for the following:

- Strictfp keyword.

- The Swing graphical API was integrated into the core classes.

- Sun's JVM was equipped with a JIT compiler.

- Java plug-in.

- Java IDL, an IDL implementation for CORBA interoperability.

- Collections framework.

J2SE 1.3 - Support for the following:

- HotSpot JVM included.

- RMI was modified to support optional compatibility with CORBA.

- Java Naming and Directory Interface (JNDI) included in core libraries.

- Java Platform Debugger Architecture (JPDA).

- JavaSound.

- Synthetic proxy classes.

J2SE 1.4 - Support for the following:

- Regular expressions modeled after Perl regular expressions.

- Exception chaining, which allows for an exception to encapsulate original lower-level exceptions.

- Internet Protocol version 6 (IPv6) support.

- Non-blocking IO.

- Logging API.

- Image I/O API for reading and writing images in formats like JPEG and PNG.

- Integrated XML parser and XSLT processor (JAXP).

- Integrated security and cryptography extensions (JCE, JSSE, JAAS).

- Java Web Start included.

- Preferences API (java.util.prefs).

J2SE 5.0 - Support for the following:

- Generics, which provides compile-time (static) type safety for collections and eliminates the need for most typecasts.

- Metadata, which is also called annotations. This allows language constructs such as classes and methods to be tagged with additional data, which can then be processed by metadata-aware utilities.

- Autoboxing/unboxing. This allows for automatic conversions between primitive types (such as int) and primitive wrapper classes (such as Integer).

- Enumerations. Here the enum keyword creates a typesafe, ordered list of values.

- Varargs. This is the last parameter of a method, which can now be declared using a type name followed by three dots.

- Enhanced 'for each' loop. The 'for' loop syntax is extended with a special syntax for iterating over each member of either an array or an Iterable, such as the standard Collection classes.

- Improved semantics of execution for multi-threaded Java programs. The new Java memory model addresses issues of complexity, effectiveness, and performance of previous specifications.

- Static imports.

Java SE 6- Support for the following:

- Scripting Language Support. A generic API is introduced for tight integration with scripting languages, and built-in Mozilla JavaScript Rhino integration.

- Dramatic performance improvements for the core platform and Swing.

- Improved Web Service support through JAX-WS.

- JDBC 4.0 support.

- Java Compiler API. This is an API allowing a Java program to select and invoke a Java Compiler programmatically.

- Upgrade of JAXB to version 2.0.

- Support for pluggable annotations.

- Many GUI improvements, such as integration of SwingWorker in the API, table sorting and filtering, and true Swing double-buffering.

- JVM improvements, which included synchronization and compiler performance optimizations, new algorithms and upgrades to existing garbage collection algorithms, and application start-up performance.

Java SE 7 - Support for the following:

- JVM support for dynamic languages, with the new invokedynamic bytecode.

- Compressed 64-bit pointers.

- Strings in the switch statement.

- Automatic resource management in the try-statement.

- Improved type inference for generic instance creation.

- Simplified varargs method declaration.

- Binary integer literals.

- Allowing underscores in numeric literals.

- Catching multiple exception types and rethrowing exceptions with improved type checking.

- New file I/O library. Here support was added for multiple file systems, file metadata and symbolic links.

- Library-level support for elliptic curve cryptography algorithms.

- An XRender pipeline for Java 2D, which improves handling of features specific to modern GPUs.

- Enhanced library-level support for new network protocols, including SCTP and Sockets Direct Protocol.

- Upstream updates to XML and Unicode.

3. Features of Java

Java has a lot of features with just a few of them mentioned below.

3.1 Simplicity

The Java language is simple to use and there are many built-in functions that are present to do most of the common jobs you need. Because the language is built specifically for the Java framework, it relies on the Java framework to do all the heavy lifting. For example, when it comes to releasing memory used by the program, you don't have to specifically do this through a Java program. It is done automatically by the garbage collector in the Java Runtime Environment

Below is a simple example of a Java program which displays 'Hello World'.

Example 4: The following program is used to showcase a simple Java program.

```
public class HelloWorld
{
    public static void main(String[] args) {
        System.out.println("Hello World!");
    }
}
```

3.2 Data Types

Java has the support for many data types. Java is a strongly typed language in which you need to define the data type of a value before it can be used. Below is a simple example of a Java program which works with data types. We will see more of this in the chapter on data types.

Example 5: The following program is used to showcase a simple Java program on data types.

```
public class HelloWorld
{
    public static void main(String[] args)
    {
        // Integer data type
        int a = 1;

        // Float data type
        float b = 1.1F;

        // String data type
        String c="Hello";

        // Character data type
        char d = 'A';

        // boolean data type
        boolean e = true;

        // Double data type
        double f = 1.11111111;

        System.out.println(" The integer data type is " + a);
        System.out.println(" The Float data type is " + b);
        System.out.println(" The String data type is " + c);
```

```
        System.out.println(" The Character data type is " + d);
        System.out.println(" The boolean data type is " + e);
        System.out.println(" The Double data type is " + f);
    }
}
```

3.3 Loops and Decision Making

Java has built-in methods that can be used to create logic based on decisions or loops to iterate through a set of values. Below is a simple example of a Java program which works with decision making and loops. We will see more of this in the chapter on decision making and loops.

Example 6: The following program is used to showcase a simple Java program on decision statements.

```
public class HelloWorld
{
    public static void main(String[] args) {

        int i = 1;
        // Decision making
        if (i == 1) { System.out.println(" The value is 1"); }

        // Loops
        for(int j=0;j<5;j++)
            System.out.println(" The value of j is " + j);
    }
}
```

3.4 Object Oriented

This is one of the basic principles of any programming language wherein one can define classes and objects. Classes are an encapsulation of properties and methods. Classes are relevant to real time entities. Below is a simple example of a Java program which works with classes. We will see more of this in book 2 of the series.

Example 7: The following program is used to showcase a simple Java program on classes.

```java
class Student
  {
    // Encapsulating the ID property
    private
      int ID;
    public void setID(int pID)
    {
      ID = pID;
    }
    public int getID()
    {
      return ID;
    }
  }

public class HelloWorld
{
   public static void main(String[] args) {

      Student stud = new Student();
      stud.setID(1);
System.out.println("The ID of the student is " +stud.getID());

   }
}
```

3.5 Data Encapsulation Support

Java has the facility to encapsulate its data members so that they are not exposed to other classes. You can then have 'getter' and 'setter' methods which can be used to get and set the data members accordingly. An example of data encapsulation is given below.

Example 8: The following program is used to showcase a simple Java program for data encapsulation.

```
class Student
  {
    // Encapsulating the ID property
    private
      int ID;
    public void setID(int pID)
    {
      ID = pID;
    }
    public int getID()
    {
      return ID;
    }
  }

public class HelloWorld
{
   public static void main(String[] args) {

      Student stud = new Student();
      stud.setID(1);
System.out.println("The ID of the student is " +stud.getID());

   }
}
```

3.6 Inheritance

Java has the support for classes to inherit the properties and methods of other classes. This greatly helps in not having the need to develop classes over and over again, and helps in better development of an application. An example of inheritance is given below. We will see this in further detail in book 2 of the series.

Example 9: The following program is used to showcase a simple Java program for inheritance.

```
class Person
  {
    // Encapsulating the ID property
    private
      int ID;
    public void setID(int pID)
    {
      ID = pID;
    }
    public int getID()
    {
      return ID;
    }
  }

class Student extends Person
  {
    private
      String Name;
    public void setName(String pName)
    {
      Name = pName;
    }
    public String getName()
```

```
   {
      return Name;
   }
 }

public class HelloWorld
{
   public static void main(String[] args) {

      Student stud = new Student();
      stud.setID(1);
      stud.setName("UserA");
System.out.println("The ID of the student is " +stud.getID());
System.out.println("The name of the student is " +stud.getName());

   }
}
```

3.7 Interfaces

An interface is a contract that a class must abide by. In an interface you have function definitions and in the class which uses the interface, you will provide information into the interface function. An example of interfaces is given below. We will see this in further detail in book 2 of the series.

Example 10: The following program is used to showcase a simple Java program for interfaces.

```
interface IStudent
  {
    // Only the function is part of the interface
    void Display();
  }
```

```java
class Student implements IStudent
  {
     // Encapsulating the ID property
     private int ID;
     private String Name;
     public void setID(int pID)
     {
       ID = pID;
     }
     public int getID()
     {
       return ID;
     }

     public void setName(String pName)
     {
       Name = pName;
     }
     public String getName()
     {
       return Name;
     }

public void Display()
{
System.out.println("The ID of the student is " +this.getID());
System.out.println("The name of the student is " +this.getName());
}
  }

public class HelloWorld
{
   public static void main(String[] args) {

       Student stud = new Student();
       stud.setID(1);
       stud.setName("UserA");
```

```
   stud.Display();
     }
}
```

3.8 Polymorphism

This is the ability of the compiler at run time, to determine the class which needs to be called. You can have a base class variable point to an object of the derived class for instance. An example of polymorphism is given below. We will see this in further detail in book 2 of the series.

Example 11: The following program is used to showcase a simple Java program for Polymorphism.

```
class Person
   {
     // Encapsulating the ID property
     private
        int ID;
     public void setID(int pID)
     {
        ID = pID;
     }
     public int getID()
     {
        return ID;
     }
public void Display()
{
  System.out.println("This is the Person class");
}
   }

class Student extends Person
```

```
    {
        private
          String Name;
        public void setName(String pName)
        {
          Name = pName;
        }
        public String getName()
        {
          return Name;
        }
public void Display()
{
  System.out.println("This is the Student class");
}
    }

public class HelloWorld
{
    public static void main(String[] args) {

    Student stud = new Student();
        Person per = new Student();
        per.Display();
        stud.Display();
    }
}
```

3.9 Collections

Java has a wide array of collections that can help reduce the
burden of writing repetitive code. With built-in classes such as
Lists, Stacks and Queues, it becomes easier to use these
classes for your application. An example of a collection is
given below. We will see this in further detail in book 3 of the
series.

Example 12: The following program is used to showcase a simple Java program for collections.

```java
import java.util.*;
public class HelloWorld
{
    public static void main(String[] args) {

Stack st = new Stack();

        // Adding elements to the stack
        st.push("A");
        st.push("B");
        st.push("C");
        st.push("D");

System.out.println(st.pop());
System.out.println(st.pop());
System.out.println(st.pop());
System.out.println(st.pop());

    }
}
```

3.10 Java Methods

This allows you to segregate code into logical pieces. An example of a collection is given below. We will look at this in further detail in book 2 of the series.

Example 13: The following program is used to showcase a simple Java program for methods.

```java
import java.util.*;
public class HelloWorld
{
public static void DisplayA()
{
    System.out.println("This displays the value A");
}
public static void DisplayB()
{
    System.out.println("This displays the value B");
}
    public static void main(String[] args) {

    DisplayA();
    DisplayB();
    }
}
```

4. The Java Compiler

The Java programming language consists of the following main components.

4.1 The Java Software Development Kit

The Java Software Development Kit is used to code your Java development language. This also contains a program known as javac, which is the Java compiler. The Java compiler is a separate program that is used to go through the Java code and break the code into smaller pieces known as symbols.

In turn, once the Java compiler has done its part, it will then pass it on the Java Interpreter. This will take the compiled code and make it into a file that can be understood by the underlying operating system. The Java Development Kit can be downloaded from the following site:

http://www.oracle.com/technetwork/java/javase/downloads/jdk8-downloads-2133151.html

4.2 The Java Runtime Environment

The Java Runtime Environment is specific to each operating system, and it is used to run the java program on the relevant operating system. Next, let's understand how the compilation process works.

Step 1

First you will write a java program and store it in a file with the .java extension. Let's take an example of the below code.

```
public class HelloWorld
{
    public static void main(String[] args) {
        System.out.println("Hello World!");
    }
}
```

We will store this in a file called HelloWorld.java. Note that the name of the file has to match the main Java class in the program.

Step 2

Next to compile the program, we will use the javac command from the java development kit. The command used to compile the program is shown below.

```
javac HelloWorld.java
```

This will compile the program and create a new class file called HelloWorld.class

Step 3

The next step is to run the program. This can be done via the java exe program. So we just run the following command.

```
java HelloWorld
```

The java program will then run on the machine. Note that we have not mentioned any extension when running the java program.

4.3 Understanding the JRE

The Java Runtime Environment, as we have seen in the earlier section, is used to run Java applications. This is an important aspect of the Java programming language. The diagram below gives a better perspective of how the Java Runtime Environment works.

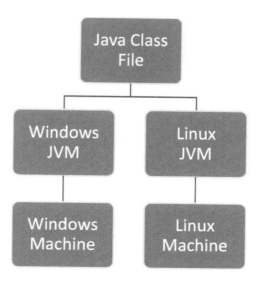

The compiler first compiles the Java program into a file with the .class extension. If you wanted to execute the java program onto a Windows machine, you would need to install the compatible Java Runtime Environment onto the Windows machine and then run the Java program. If you wanted to execute the Java program onto a Linux machine, you would need to install the specific Java Runtime Environment for Linux.

Below is the link for the Java Runtime Environment downloads for the various operating systems.

http://www.oracle.com/technetwork/java/javase/downloads/jre8-downloads-2133155.html

4.4 Different Java Editions

Java has many editions. The different editions and what they stand for are briefly discussed below:

- The Java Standard Platform Edition – This is the core Java platform. This is what provides the Java programming API, which are the different programs that compile and run Java programs. Here you get access to the core classes, such as the system classes, networking, security, database access and graphical user interfaces.

- Java Enterprise Edition – This is mostly used for developing and supporting applications on a major scale. It's primarily targeted at large organizations that need to develop application on multiple tiers and multiple platforms. Here you can build more scalable, reliable, and secure network applications.

- Java Micro Edition – This is a smaller subset of the Java programming language and is used to develop application for smaller devices such as mobile phones and tablets.

- Java FX - JavaFX is a platform for creating rich internet applications using a lightweight user interface API. This API can make use of high level graphic processors to create more appealing applications to the end users.

5. Building Your Environment

In order to start working with creating Java programs, you need to get the following in place.

5.1 Installing the Java Development Kit

The Java Development Kit, or JDK, is used to develop Java based programs. The JDK has all the necessary supporting code to help in developing Java based applications. It is released by Oracle, who continues to make improvements and revisions based on fixes reported by developers or end users. The link for the Java Development Kit can be found below.

http://www.oracle.com/technetwork/java/javase/downloads/jdk8-downloads-2133151.html

Once the Java Development Kit is installed, the next step is to ensure that it is installed properly. The easiest way to do this, is to issue the following command.

```
java -version
```

A sample output is given below. It will show the Java version that is installed on the system.

java version "1.8.0_101"

Java(TM) SE Runtime Environment (build 1.8.0_101-b13)

Java HotSpot(TM) 64-Bit Server VM (build 25.101-b13, mixed mode)

5.2 Writing Programs in Editors

To write programs, you use a simple editor such as Notepad or you can use a full-fledged Integrated Development Environment (IDE). Below is a list of some of the most popular IDE's that are available for Java and some of their relevant features.

5.2.1 Eclipse

This IDE has been around for quite a long time and is very popular and widely used amongst the Java development community. Some of the core features of the IDE are:

- It's free and open source. Hence there are many developers who keep contributing to the IDE.

- It can be used to develop applications in other languages such as C++, Ruby, HTML5 and PHP.

- It has a rich client platform.

- It provides the ability of refactoring code.

- It helps in code completion.

- It has a wide variety of extensions and plugins.

- It also has support for most source code version control systems.

The official link for Eclipse is www.eclipse.org

5.2.2 IntelliJ IDEA

This is another popular IDE used by the Java development community. Some of the core features of this IDE are:

- The community edition is free and open source.

- The paid edition provides much more features and allows developers to build enterprise applications with the Java Enterprise Edition.

- It provides the ability of refactoring code.

- It helps in code completion.

- It has a wide variety of extensions and plugins.

- It also has support for most source code version control systems.

The official link for IntelliJ IDEA is https://www.jetbrains.com/idea

5.2.3 NetBeans

This IDE can also be used to develop all sorts of Java based applications, right from Java standard programs to enterprise and mobile based applications. Some of the core features of the IDE are:

- With its editors, code analyzers, and converters you can quickly and smoothly upgrade your applications to use new Java language constructs, such as lambdas, functional operations, and method references.

- Batch analyzers and converters are provided to search through multiple applications at the same time, matching patterns for conversion to new Java language constructs.

- NetBeans IDE provides different views of your data, from multiple project windows to helpful tools for setting up your applications and managing them efficiently.

- It also has support for most source code version control systems.

The official link for NetBeans is https://netbeans.org

Below is a snapshot of how a Java Program would be created in an IntelliJ IDEA Community Edition environment.

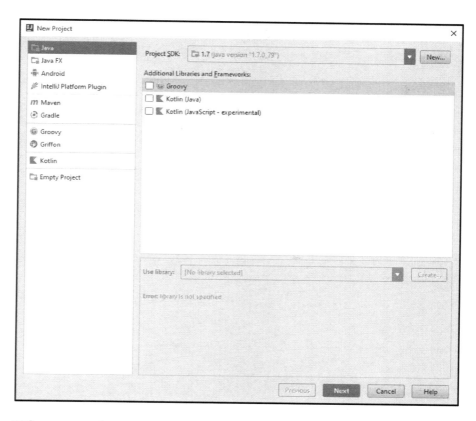

When creating a new project, you would choose the Java environment, as well as the Project SDK that would be linked to the Java SDK installed in your machine. Once you give a name to the project, you can then choose to create a new Java class.

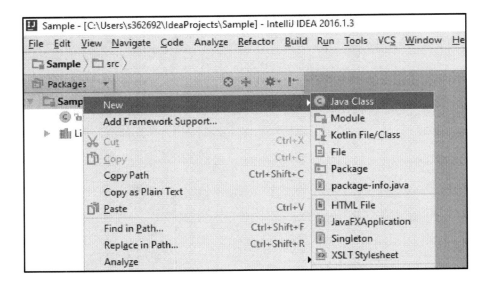

Once the class is created, you can then edit the program in the editor

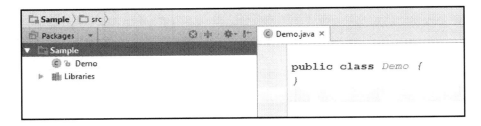

6. Your First Java Program

Let's dive into your first Java program. We have already seen in the previous chapter how to get the entire Java setup in place. It's now time to develop your first "Hello World" program. Below is the code you need to enter.

Example 14: The following program is used to showcase a simple Hello World program.

```
// This is a Java class
public class Demo
{
    // This is the main entry point of the Java program
    public static void main(String args[])
    {
        // Here we are printing Hello world to the console
        System.out.println("Hello World");
    }
}
```

With this program, the output is as follows:

Hello World

Now let's break the program down into multiple steps to understand each statement.

1) public class Demo;

This statement is used to define the class for the code. All Java code must reside in a class. It is the code in this class which gets executed. The name of the main class should also be the same name as the file which holds the class.

2) public static void main(String args[])

This is the main entry point for the Java program. The code will start executing from this function. That is why this is called as the main function. The function does not return any values, hence it has the void prefix. You can pass arguments when calling the main java program. This will be available in the args[] parameter.

3) // This is a Java class

This is a way to add a comment to the program. Comments are good for documentation purposes and help to maintain the code for the future.

4) System.out.println("Hello World");

Finally we are using the String.out.println function to print Hello World to the console.

So now we have seen how to write our first program. Let's look at another example, but this time let's look at using a variable.

Example 15: The following program is used to showcase how you can write your second program.

```java
// This is a Java class
public class Demo
{
   // This is the main entry point of the Java program
   public static void main(String args[])
   {
      // Initializing a variable
      int i=5;

      // Displaying the variable

      System.out.println("The value of i is "+i);
   }
}
```

With this program, the output is as follows:

The value of i is 5

Let's look at the changes we made in this program.

1) int i=5;

Here we have declared a variable called 'i' and assigned a value of 5 to this variable. There is a separate chapter on variables and data types, but to get the hang of how to start using variables, you can experiment with the above program.

2) System.out.println("The value of i is "+i);

Now we are working towards displaying the value of our variable. We are still using our System.out.println function. But here we are combining the string "The value of i is" and the value of 'i' itself. This can be done with the help of the + operator.

Now let's look at a similar program to the one shown above, but with a small change to the program.

Example 16: The following program is used to showcase how you can write your third program.

```java
// This is a Java class
public class Demo
{
    // This is the main entry point of the Java program
    public static void main(String args[])
    {
        // Initializing a variable
        int i=5;

        // Displaying the variable

        System.out.println("The value of i is "+i);

        // We are incrementing the value of i by one

        i=i+1;

        System.out.println("The value of i is "+i);
    }
}
```

With this program, the output is as follows:

The value of i is 5

The value of i is 6

Let's look at the changes we made in this program.

1) i=i+1

Here we are merely incrementing the value of 'i' by one. We are then assigning the incremented value back to 'i' again.

Great, we have seen our first few programs. Now you are ready to work with a few more advanced topics in the following chapters.

7. Data Types

Data types are used in programming languages to store different types of data. For example if you wanted to store text data, you would probably have a data type of 'string'. If you wanted to store a number you can have a data type of say 'number' or 'integer'. This depends on the programming language and what data types are defined. Data types help to make the program type safe and free from errors.

Now let's look at the different data types available in Java.

Table 1: Data Types

Data Type	Description	Range (bits)
byte	This is an 8-bit signed two complement integer	-128 to 127
short	This is a 16-bit signed two complement integer	-32,768 to 32,767

Data Type	Description	Range (bits)
int	This is a 32-bit signed two complement integer	-2,147,483,648 to 2,147,483,647
long	This is a 64-bit signed two complement integer	-9223372036854775808 to 9223372036854775807
float	This is a single-precision 32-bit IEEE 754 floating point	-3.402823e38 to 3.402823e38
double	This is a double-precision 64-bit IEEE 754 floating point	-1.79769313486232e308 to 1.79769313486232e308
char	This is a single 16-bit Unicode character	0 to 65,535
boolean	This has only two possible values: true and false	8
string	This is used to define a sequence of characters	N/A

46

Next we will discuss each data type in more detail with the help of a Java program for each data type. Remember to try these out yourself to help better understand the concepts.

7.1 Byte Data Type

This data type is used to define an unsigned integer, which can have a range of values from -128 to 127.

Example 17: The following program is used to showcase the byte data type.

```
// This is a Java class
public class Demo
{
    // This is the main entry point of the Java program
    public static void main(String args[])
    {
        // Initializing a variable
        byte i=5;

        // Displaying the variable
        System.out.println("The byte value is "+i);
    }
}
```

With this program, the output is as follows:

The byte value is 5

7.2 Short Data Type

This data type is used to define a short data type, which is a 16-bit signed two complement integer with a range of -32,768 to 32,767.

Example 18: The following program is used to showcase the short data type.

```java
// This is a Java class
public class Demo
{
    // This is the main entry point of the Java program
    public static void main(String args[])
    {
        // Initializing a variable
        short i=5;
        short j=-6;

        // Displaying the variable
        System.out.println("The value of i is "+i);
        System.out.println("The value of j is "+j);
    }
}
```

With this program, the output is as follows:

The value of i is 5

The value of j is -6

7.3 Int Data Type

This data type is used to define a signed integer, which has a range of values from -2,147,483,648 to 2,147,483,647.

Example 19: The following program is used to showcase the int data type.

```java
// This is a Java class
public class Demo
{
  // This is the main entry point of the Java program
  public static void main(String args[])
  {
    // Initializing a variable
    int i=5;
    int j=-6;

    // Displaying the variable
    System.out.println("The value of i is "+i);
    System.out.println("The value of j is "+j);
  }
}
```

With this program, the output is as follows:

The value of i is 5

The value of j is -6

7.4 Long Data Type

This data type is used to define a 64-bit signed two complement integer, which has a range of values from -9223372036854775808 to 9223372036854775807.

Example 20: The following program is used to showcase the long data type.

```java
// This is a Java class
public class Demo
{
    // This is the main entry point of the Java program
    public static void main(String args[])
    {
        // Initializing a variable
        long i = 100000000;
        long j = -45000000;

        // Displaying the variable
        System.out.println("The value of i is "+i);
        System.out.println("The value of j is "+j);
    }
}
```

With this program, the output is as follows:

The value of i is 100000000

The value of j is 45000000

7.5 Float Data Type

This data type is used to define a single-precision floating point type, which has a range of values from -3.402823e38 to 3.402823e38.

Example 21: The following program is used to showcase the float data type.

```java
// This is a Java class
public class Demo
{
    // This is the main entry point of the Java program
    public static void main(String args[])
    {
        // Initializing a variable
        float i = 10.11F;
        float j = -45.44F;

        // Displaying the variable
        System.out.println("The value of i is "+i);
        System.out.println("The value of j is "+j);
    }
}
```

With this program, the output is as follows:

The value of i is 10.11

The value of j -45.44

7.6 Double Data Type

This data type is used to define a double-precision floating point type, which has a range of values from $-1.79769313486232e308$ to $1.79769313486232e308$.

Example 22: The following program is used to showcase the double data type.

```java
// This is a Java class
public class Demo
{
    // This is the main entry point of the Java program
    public static void main(String args[])
    {
        // Initializing a variable
        double i = 10.11111111;
        double j = -45.4444444;

        // Displaying the variable
        System.out.println("The value of i is "+i);
        System.out.println("The value of j is "+j);
    }
}
```

With this program, the output is as follows:

The value of i is 10.11111111

The value of j is -45.4444444

7.7 Char Data Type

This data type is used to define a single Unicode character.

Example 23: The following program is used to showcase the char data type.

```java
// This is a Java class
public class Demo
{
    // This is the main entry point of the Java program
```

```
  public static void main(String args[])
  {
    // Initializing a variable
    char i = 'A';
    char j = 'a';

    // Displaying the variable
    System.out.println("The value of i is "+i);
    System.out.println("The value of j is "+j);
  }
}
```

With this program, the output is as follows:

The value of i is A

The value of j is a

7.8 Boolean Data Type

This data type is used to define a Boolean value, which can either be true or false.

Example 24: The following program is used to showcase the Boolean data type.

```
// This is a Java class
public class Demo
{
  // This is the main entry point of the Java program
  public static void main(String args[])
  {
    // Initializing a variable
    boolean i = true;
    boolean j = false;
```

```
// Displaying the variable
System.out.println("The value of i is "+i);
System.out.println("The value of j is "+j);
}
}
```

With this program, the output is as follows:

The value of i is True

The value of j is False

7.9 String Data Type

This data type is used to define a sequence of characters.

Example 25: The following program is used to showcase the string data type.

```
// This is a Java class
public class Demo
{
    // This is the main entry point of the Java program
    public static void main(String args[])
    {
        // Initializing a variable
        String i = "Hello";
        String j = "World";

        // Displaying the variable
        System.out.println("The value of i is "+i);
        System.out.println("The value of j is "+j);
    }
}
```

With this program, the output is as follows:

The value of i is Hello

The value of j is World

7.10 Default Values for Fields

If no values are defined for fields in the various data types, they are assigned their default values. We will discuss fields in detail when we cover classes in book 2 of the series, but it's good to have a basic understanding at this point. The table below provides the default values for the various data types.

Table 2: Data Types Default Values

Data Type	Default Value
byte	0
short	0
int	0
long	0L
float	0.0f
double	0.0d
char	'\u000'
string	null
boolean	false

8. Variables

Variables are used to define values which can be changed during the course of the program. You can have different types of variables based on the various data types. Let's look at the different types of variables we can create based on their data type.

8.1 Character Variables

These are variables that are used to hold characters, which can be changed at any point in time in the program. Let's look at an example of a character variable.

Example 26: The following program is used to showcase character variables.

```java
// This is a Java class
public class Demo
{
    // This is the main entry point of the Java program
    public static void main(String args[])
    {
        // Initializing a variable
        char i='A';

        // Displaying the variable
        System.out.println("The value of i is "+i);
```

```
    i='B';
    System.out.println("The value of i is "+i);

  }
}
```

With this program, the output is as follows:

The value is i is A

The value is i is B

8.2 Integer Variables

These are variables that are used to hold integers, which can be changed at any point in time in the program. Let's look at an example of an integer variable.

Example 27: The following program is used to showcase integer variables.

```
// This is a Java class
public class Demo
{
  // This is the main entry point of the Java program
  public static void main(String args[])
  {
    // Initializing a variable
    int i=5;

    // Displaying the variable
    System.out.println("The value of i is "+i);
    i=6;
    System.out.println("The value of i is "+i);
  }
}
```

With this program, the output is as follows:

The value is i is 5

The value is i is 6

8.3 Floating Point Variables

These variables are used to hold floating point numbers, which can of course be changed at any point in time within the program. Let's look at an example of a floating point variable.

Example 28: The following program is used to showcase floating point variables.

```java
// This is a Java class
public class Demo
{
  // This is the main entry point of the Java program
  public static void main(String args[])
  {
    // Initializing a variable
   float i=1.11F;

    // Displaying the variable
    System.out.println("The value of i is "+i);
    i=2.22F;
    System.out.println("The value of i is "+i);

  }
}
```

With this program, the output is as follows:

The value of i is 1.11

The value of i is 2.22

8.4 Double Point Variables

These are variables that are used to hold double point numbers, which can be changed at any point in time in the program. Let's look at an example of a double point variable.

Example 29: The following program is used to showcase double point variables.

```java
// This is a Java class
public class Demo
{
    // This is the main entry point of the Java program
    public static void main(String args[])
    {
        // Initializing a variable
        double i=1.11111;

        // Displaying the variable
        System.out.println("The value of i is "+i);
        i=2.22222;
        System.out.println("The value of i is "+i);

    }
}
```

With this program, the output is as follows:

The value of i is 1.11111

The value of i is 2.22222

8.5 String Variables

These are variables used to hold strings, which can be changed at any point in time within the program. Let's look at an example of a string variable.

Example 30: The following program is used to showcase string variables.

```java
// This is a Java class
public class Demo
{
   // This is the main entry point of the Java program
   public static void main(String args[])
   {
     // Initializing a variable
    String i="Hello";

     // Displaying the variable
     System.out.println("The value of i is "+i);
     i="World";
     System.out.println("The value of i is "+i);

   }
}
```

With this program, the output is as follows:

The value of i is Hello

The value of i is World

8.6 Boolean Variables

These variables are used to hold Booleans, which can of course be changed at any point during the program. Let's look at an example of a Boolean variable.

Example 31: The following program is used to showcase Boolean variables.

```java
// This is a Java class
public class Demo
{
    // This is the main entry point of the Java program
    public static void main(String args[])
    {
        // Initializing a variable
        Boolean i=true;

        // Displaying the variable
        System.out.println("The value of i is "+i);
        i=false;
        System.out.println("The value of i is "+i);

    }
}
```

With this program, the output is as follows:

The value of i is true

The value of i is False

8.7 Variables Scope

Variables also have a defined scope and this depends on where they are defined in a program. Let's take the sample block of code given below.

```
public static void main(String args[])
{
   int a;
}
```

Here 'a' is defined in the beginning of the main function and hence has a global scope. This means it can be used anywhere in the program. But now let's look at another example of variable declaration.

```
public static void main(String args[])
{
{
   // Inner Scope
   int a;
}
   // Integer a cannot be used here
}
```

In the above example, the variable 'a' is now limited to the second curly braces and cannot be accessed outside the Inner Scope curly braces. The scope of integer 'a' is now private to the block of code inside the second curly braces. Let's now look at an example on using variables defined by a particular scope.

Example 32: The following program is used to show variable scope.

```java
import java.io.Console;

// This is a Java class
public class Demo
{
   // This is the main entry point of the Java program
   public static void main(String args[])
   {
     int i=5; // Outer Scope
     System.out.println("The value of i is "+i);
     {
       int j=6; // Inner Scope
       System.out.println("The value of j is "+j);
     }
   }
}
```

With this program, the output is as follows:.

The value of i is 5

The value of j is 6

Let's look at the same example and try to create an error in the program to confirm our understanding of scope variables.

Example 33: The following program is used to show the wrong way to use variables scope.

```java
import java.io.Console;

// This is a Java class
public class Demo
```

```
{
  // This is the main entry point of the Java program
  public static void main(String args[])
  {
    int i=5; // Outer Scope
    System.out.println("The value of i is "+i);
    {
      int j=6; // Inner Scope
      System.out.println("The value of j is "+j);
    }
    System.out.println("The value of j is "+j);
  }
}
```

With this program, you will actually get a compile time error.

Error:(15, 49) java: cannot find symbol

symbol: variable j

location: class Demo

As rightly so, there is an error in the program because we are trying to use the value of 'j' outside the scope in which it is defined.

9. Constants

A constant is an identifier whose value does not change during the course of the program. For example, if you were to define an identifier with a name of 'val', assign a value of 5 to it, and also define it as a constant value, then you would not be able to change the value of that identifier.

In Java, the syntax for defining a constant is shown below.

```
static final datatype identifier = value
```

Where:

- Static is a keyword which means that the variable is available without the need of having to define an instance of the class.

- The final keyword is used to denote that the value assigned to the identifier cannot be changed during the course of the program.

Let's now at an example of how we can define constants in a program.

Example 34: The following program is used to show how to define constants.

```java
// This is a Java class
public class Demo
{
    static final int i=5;

    // This is the main entry point of the Java program
    public static void main(String args[])

    {
        System.out.println("The value of i is "+i);
    }
}
```

With this program, the output is as follows:

The value of i is 5

Now let's write the same program, but this time try to change the value of 'i' during the course of the program.

Example 35: The following program is used to show the wrong way to work with constants.

```java
// This is a Java class
public class Demo
{
    static final int i=5;
    // This is the main entry point of the Java program
    public static void main(String args[])
    {
        System.out.println("The value of i is "+i);
```

```
        i++;
    }
}
```

With this program, you will get a compile time error as shown below.

Error:(10, 9) java: cannot assign a value to final variable i

We can define multiple constants in a program and we can also use them alongside normal variables. Let's look at another example of how we can use constants.

Example 36: The following program is used to show another example of constants.

```
// This is a Java class
public class Demo
{
    static final int ValA=5;
    static final int ValB=5;
    // This is the main entry point of the Java program
    public static void main(String args[])
    {
        int ValC=ValA+ValB;
        System.out.println("The value of ValC is "+ValC);
    }
}
```

In the above program we are carrying out the following steps:

- First we are defining 2 constants – ValA and ValB.

- We then use them in an operation with a normal variable ValC. We are just performing a simple addition operation.

With this program, the output is as follows:

The value of ValC is 5

10. Operators

There are various types of operators available in Java. The operators help in carrying out various operations on the defined variables in a Java program. Let's look at each of the operators in more detail.

10.1 Arithmetic Operators

These are operators that are used when working with numbers. The most common operators are shown below, with an example of them in action in one program.

Table 3: Arithmetic Operators

Operator	Operation
+	This is used to add two operands
-	This is used to subtract one operand from another
*	This is used to multiply two operands
/	This is used to divide one operand by another

Operator	Operation
%	This gives a percentage value after a division operator
++	This is used to increment a value by one
--	This is used to decrement a value by one

Example 37: The following program shows the way we can use arithmetic operators.

```java
// This is a Java class
public class Demo
{
    // This is the main entry point of the Java program
    public static void main(String args[])
    {
        int i=4;
        int j=5;

        //The addition of the two operands
        System.out.println("The addition of the two operands is " +
(i+j));

        //The subtraction of the two operands
        System.out.println("The subtraction of the two operands is " +
(i - j));

        //The multiplication of the two operands
        System.out.println("The multiplication of the two operands is "
+ (i * j));

        //The division of the two operands
        System.out.println("The division of the two operands is " + (i /
j));
```

```
    //The remainder after division of the two operands
    System.out.println("The remainder after division of the two
operands is " + (i % j));

    //Incrementing operand one by one
    System.out.println("Incrementing operand one by one " +
(++i));

    //Decrementing operand two by one
    System.out.println("Decrementing operand two by one " + (--
j));
  }
}
```

With this program, the output is as follows:

The addition of the two operands is 9

The subtraction of the two operands is -1

The multiplication of the two operands is 20

The division of the two operands is 0

The remainder after division of the two operands is 4

Incrementing operand one by one 5

Decrementing operand two by one 4

10.2 Relational Operators

These are operators that are used to determine the value of conditions based on the value of the operands. The relational operators possible in Java are given below, with all of them used in an example.

Table 4: Relational Operators

Operator	Operation
==	This is used to check if two operands are equal
!=	This is used to check if two operands are not equal
>	This is used to check if one operand is greater than another
<	This is used to check if one operand is less than another
>=	This is used to check if one operand is greater than or equal to another
<=	This is used to check if one operand is less than or equal to another

If a condition evaluates to true, then a value of 1 is returned else a value of 0 is returned.

Example 38: The following program shows the way we can use relational operators.

```
// This is a Java class
public class Demo
{
    // This is the main entry point of the Java program
    public static void main(String args[])
    {
        int i=4;
        int j=5;
```

```
    //Is i equal to j
    System.out.println("Is i equal to j  " + (i==j));

    //Is i not equal to j
    System.out.println("Is i not equal to j  " + (i!=j));

    //Is i greater than j
    System.out.println("Is i greater than j  " + (i>j));

    //Is i less than j
    System.out.println("Is i less than j  " + (i<j));

    //Is i greater than or equal j
    System.out.println("Is i greater than or equal j  " + (i>=j));

    //Is i less than or equal j
    System.out.println("Is i less than or equal j " + (i<=j));
  }
}
```

With this program, the output is as follows:

Is i equal to j false
Is i not equal to j true
Is i greater than j false
Is i less than j true
Is i greater than or equal j false
Is i less than or equal j true

10.3 Logical Operators

These are operators that are used to determine the value of conditions based on the value of the operands, where the operands are Boolean values. The logical operators possible in Java are given below.

Table 5: Relational Operators

Operator	Operation
&&	This is the logical AND operator
||	This is the logical OR operator
!	This is the Logical NOT operator

Below is a table for the logical operators based on the value of the operands for the AND operator, as well as an example of the different results.

Table 5.1: Relational Operators - AND

Operand A	Operand B	Result
True	True	1
True	False	0
False	True	0
False	False	0

Example 39: The following program shows how to use logical operators for the AND operator.

```
// This is a Java class
public class Demo
{
    // This is the main entry point of the Java program
    public static void main(String args[])
    {
```

```
        boolean i = true;
        boolean j = true;
        boolean k = false;

        //i AND j
        System.out.println("i AND j  " + (i&&j));

        //i AND k
        System.out.println("i AND k  " + (i&&k));

        //k AND i
        System.out.println("k AND i  " + (k&&i));

        //k AND k
        System.out.println("k AND k  " + (k&&k));
    }
}
```

With this program, the output is as follows:

i AND j true

i AND k false

k AND i false

k AND k false

Below is a table for the logical operators based on the value of
the operands for the OR operator, followed by an example.

Table 5.2: Relational Operators - OR

Operand A	Operand B	Result
True	True	1
True	False	1

Operand A	Operand B	Result
False	True	1
False	False	0

Example 40: The following program shows how to use logical operators for the OR operator.

```java
// This is a Java class
public class Demo
{
    // This is the main entry point of the Java program
    public static void main(String args[])
    {
        boolean i = true;
        boolean j = true;
        boolean k = false;

        //i OR j
        System.out.println("i OR j   " + (i||j));

        //i OR k
        System.out.println("i AND k   " + (i||k));

        //k OR i
        System.out.println("k OR i   " + (k||i));

        //k OR k
        System.out.println("k OR k  " + (k||k));
    }
}
```

With this program, the output is as follows:

i OR j   true

i AND k   true

k OR i   true

k OR k   false

Last is a table for the logical operators based on the value of the operands for the NOT operator with an example showing the different results.

Table 5.3: Relational Operators - NOT

Operand A	Result
True	0
False	1

Example 41: The following program shows how to use logical operators for the NOT operator.

```
// This is a Java class
public class Demo
{
   // This is the main entry point of the Java program
   public static void main(String args[])
   {
     boolean i = true;
     boolean j = false;

     //NOT i
     System.out.println("NOT i   " + (!i));
```

```
    //NOT j
    System.out.println("NOT j   " + (!j));
  }
}
```

With this program, the output is as follows:

NOT i   false

NOT j   true

10.4 Assignment Operators

These are operators that are used to make assignment
operations easier. The assignment operators possible in Java
are given below.

Table 6: Assignment Operators

Operator	Operation
=	This is used to assign the value of an operation to an operand
+=	This is used to carry out the addition and assignment operator in one go
-=	This is used to carry out the subtraction and assignment operator in one go
*=	This is used to carry out the multiplication and assignment operator in one go
/=	This is used to carry out the division and assignment operator in one go

Operator	Operation
%=	This is used to carry out the modulus and assignment operator in one go

Now let's look at how we can implement these operators in further detail through an example showcasing all the operators.

Example 42: The following program shows the way we can use assignment operators.

```java
// This is a Java class
public class Demo
{
  // This is the main entry point of the Java program
  public static void main(String args[])
  {
    int i = 5;
    int j = 10;

    //The value of i+j
    System.out.println("The value of i+j is " + (i+j));

    //The value of i+=j
    System.out.println("The value of i+=j is  " + (i+=j));

    //The value of i+=j
    System.out.println("The value of i-=j is  " + (i -= j));

    //The value of i*=j
    System.out.println("The value of i*=j is  " + (i *= j));

    //The value of i/=j is
    System.out.println("The value of i/=j is  " + (i /= j));
```

```
    //The value of i%=j is
    System.out.println("The value of i%=j is   " + (i %= j));
  }
}
```

With this program, the output is as follows:

The value of i+j is 15

The value of i+=j is 15

The value of i-=j is 5

The value of i*=j is 50

The value of i/=j is 5

The value of i%=j is 5

10.5 Bitwise Operators

These are operators that are used to make bit operations on operands. The assignment operators possible in Java are given below with an example of them in action.

Table 7: Bitwise Operators

Operator	Operation
&	This copies a bit to the result if it exists in both operands
|	This copies a bit to the result if it exists in either operands
^	This copies a bit to the result if it exists in one operand but not in both

Operator	Operation
<<	Here the left operands value is moved left by the number of bits specified by the right operand
>>	Here the left operands value is moved right by the number of bits specified by the right operand

Example 43: The following program shows the way we can use bitwise operators.

```
// This is a Java class
public class Demo
{
    // This is the main entry point of the Java program
    public static void main(String args[])
    {
        int i = 5;
        int j = 10;

        //Showcasing the & bit operator
        System.out.println("Showcasing the & bit operator  " + (i&j));

        //Showcasing the | bit operator
        System.out.println("Showcasing the | bit operator  " + (i|j));

        //Showcasing the ^ bit operator
        System.out.println("Showcasing the ^ bit operator  " + (i^j));

        //Showcasing the << bit operator
        System.out.println("Showcasing the << bit operator   " +
(i<<2));
```

```
   //Showcasing the >> bit operator
    System.out.println("Showcasing the >> bit operator    " +
(i>>j));
  }
}
```

With this program, the output is as follows:

Showcasing the & bit operator 0

Showcasing the | bit operator 15

Showcasing the ^ bit operator 15

Showcasing the << bit operator 20

Showcasing the >> bit operator 0

11. Type Conversion

The Java programming language allows type conversion between primitive types. This allows the conversion from one data type to another. There are 2 types of conversions, one is called implicit and the other, explicit. We will discuss implicit conversion first. Here the java compiler performs the type conversion if it is not mentioned in the program.

Below is an example of an implicit conversion.

```
char valA='a';
int valB=valA;
```

In the first statement, we are assigning the character value of 'a' to an identifier of valA. In the second statement, even though we declare a variable of the type integer, we are still able to assign the variable of the type character to this. This conversion is done directly by the compiler.

Type conversions should always be done with caution as it can have unknown consequences in the output of the program. The following primitive types can undergo type conversion:

- char

- byte

- short

- int

- long

- float

- double

Now let's look at an example on how we can work with implicit conversions.

Example 44: The following program is used to showcase the implicit type conversion.

```java
// This is a Java class
public class Demo
{
  // This is the main entry point of the Java program
  public static void main(String args[])
  {
    char valA='a';
    // Carrying out the type case operation
    int valB = valA;

    System.out.println("The value of valA is "+ valA);
    System.out.println("The value of valB is "+ valB);
  }
}
```

With this program, the output is as follows:

The value of valA is a

The value of valB is 97

In the output you can see that the character value is converted to its equivalent ASCII value when being taken as an integer. Let's see another example with floating and double precision numbers.

Example 45: The following program is used to show the implicit type conversion with numbers.

```java
// This is a Java class
public class Demo
{
    // This is the main entry point of the Java program
    public static void main(String args[])
    {
        float valA=5.55f;
        // Carrying out the type case operation
        double valB = valA;

        System.out.println("The value of valA is "+ valA);
        System.out.println("The value of valA is "+ valB);
    }
}
```

With this program, the output is as follows:

The value of valA is 5.55

The value of valA is 5.550000190734863

There is one thing to note when it comes to conversion. In the above example, we called on the Java compiler to carry out an implicit type conversion from floating point number to double.

But the reverse cannot be done. This is because we cannot ask the compiler to convert a bigger byte data type to a smaller one. And since the double data type can hold more digits, we cannot convert it to a floating number using implicit conversion. So let's try this out and see what happens.

Example 46: The following program shows an illegal implicit type conversion with numbers.

```
// This is a Java class
public class Demo
{
    // This is the main entry point of the Java program
    public static void main(String args[])
    {
        double valA=5.55;
        // Carrying out the type case operation
        float valB = valA;

        System.out.println("The value of valA is "+ valA);
        System.out.println("The value of valA is "+ valB);
    }
}
```

With this program, you would actually get a compile time error.

Error:(9, 22) java: possible loss of precision

required: float

found: double

We can overcome the above problem by using the next type of conversion which is called explicit conversion. This is where we specifically tell the compiler to carry out the conversion. Let's look at how we can achieve this via an example.

Example 47: The following program shows an illegal implicit type conversion with numbers.

```
// This is a Java class
public class Demo
{
    // This is the main entry point of the Java program
    public static void main(String args[])
    {
        double valA=5.55;
        // Carrying out the type case operation
        float valB = (float)valA;

        System.out.println("The value of valA is "+ valA);
        System.out.println("The value of valA is "+ valB);
    }
}
```

In the above program we need to note the following:

- In the statement 'float valB = (float)valA', we are now explicitly telling the compiler to perform the cast. This will force the Java compiler to carry out the conversion.

With this program, the output is as follows:

The value of valA is 5.55

The value of valA is 5.55

12. Loops

The usage of loops helps us to iterate through a set of values. Let's say you wanted to go through a list of students and display their names. Loops can help you iterate through the list of students easily and can help access each record separately. Loops work on a condition and only execute the code based on the condition. A simple view of how this works is shown below.

```
Loop(condition)
{
//Execute code
}
```

In the above abstract code snippet, we can see that the code will be executed based on the evaluation of the condition in the loop statement. There are different types of loop statement and in this chapter we will go through each of the available loop types in more detail.

12.1 While Loops

The general syntax of the while loop is given below.

```
While(condition)
{
//execute code
}
```

As long as the condition is true in the 'while' loop, the code in the 'while' code block will continue to execute. Let's look at an example of the 'while' statement.

Example 48: The following program is used to showcase how to use the while loop.

```java
// This is a Java class
public class Demo
{
  // This is the main entry point of the Java program
  public static void main(String args[])
  {
    int i=0;
    while(i<4)
    {
      System.out.println("The value of i is "+ i);
      i++;
    }
  }
}
```

Things to note about the above program:

- We are defining an integer 'i' which has an initial value of 1.

- In the while loop we state the condition that while the value of 'i' is less than 4, keep on executing the code in the while code block.

- In the while code block, we display the value of 'i' and also increment the value of i.

With this program, the output is as follows:

The value of i is 0

The value of i is 1

The value of i is 2

The value of i is 3

12.2 Do-While Loops

The general syntax of the 'do-while' loop is given below.

```
do
{
//execute code
}
While(condition);
```

Here the difference between the 'do-while' loop and the normal 'while' loop is that the condition is tested at the end of the block of code. This means that you will always be guaranteed that the block of code will be executed at least once. Let's look at an example of the 'do-while' statement.

Example 49: The following program is used to showcase how to use the do-while loop.

```
// This is a Java class
public class Demo
{
    // This is the main entry point of the Java program
    public static void main(String args[])
    {
        int i=0;
        do
```

```
    {
        System.out.println("The value of i is "+ i);
        i++;
    }
    while(i<4);
  }
}
```

With this program, the output is as follows:

The value of i is 0

The value of i is 1

The value of i is 2

The value of i is 3

12.3 For Loops

The general syntax of the 'for' loop is given below.

```
for(initialization;condition;incrementer)
{
//execute code
}
```

In the 'for' clause, you can specify the initialization, condition and incrementer in one statement. Let's look at an example of the 'for' loop statement.

Example 50: The following program is used to showcase how to use the for loop.

```java
// This is a Java class
public class Demo
{
  // This is the main entry point of the Java program
  public static void main(String args[])
  {
    for(int i=0;i<4;i++)
    {
      System.out.println("The value of i is "+ i);
    }
  }
}
```

Things to note about the above program:

- We are now initializing the value of 'i' in the for loop itself.

- We are also testing for the condition of the value of 'i' in the for loop itself.

- Next we are incrementing the value of 'i' in the for loop itself.

With this program, the output is as follows:

The value of i is 0

The value of i is 1

The value of i is 2

The value of i is 3

12.4 Nested Loops

We can also nest loops one inside of another. Let's look at some examples of nested loops.

Example 51: The following program is used to showcase how to use nested loops.

```java
// This is a Java class
public class Demo
{
  // This is the main entry point of the Java program
  public static void main(String args[])
  {
    for(int i=0;i<3;i++)
    {
      System.out.println("The value of i is "+ i);
      for(int j=0;j<3;j++)
      {
        System.out.println("The value of j is "+ j);
      }
    }
  }
}
```

With this program, the output is as follows:

The value of i is 0

The value of j is 0

The value of j is 1

The value of j is 2

The value of i is 1

The value of j is 0

The value of j is 1

The value of j is 2

The value of i is 2

The value of j is 0

The value of j is 1

The value of j is 2

Let's see another example on how we can use nested loops.

Example 52: The following program is used to showcase how to use nested loops.

```java
// This is a Java class
public class Demo
{
   // This is the main entry point of the Java program
   public static void main(String args[])
   {
      for(int i=0;i<3;i++)
      {
         System.out.println("The value of i is "+ i);
         int j=0;
         while(j<3)
         {
            System.out.println("The value of j is "+ j);
            j++;
         }
      }
   }
}
```

With this program, the output is as follows:

The value of i is 0

The value of j is 0

The value of j is 1

The value of j is 2

The value of i is 1

The value of j is 0

The value of j is 1

The value of j is 2

The value of i is 2

The value of j is 0

The value of j is 1

The value of j is 2

13. Decision Making

The use of decision making loops helps us to execute code only if a particular condition holds true. Let says we wanted to search for records in a student database and only award scholarships to those students whose aggregate marks were above 90%, we could use decision loops for this purpose.

A sample decision loop structure is shown below.

```
if(condition)
{
//Execute code
}
```

In the above abstract code snippet, we can see that the code will be executed based on the evaluation of the condition in the 'if' statement. Only if the condition is true, will the code block statements be executed. There are different types of decision making statements and in this chapter we will go through each of the available statements in more detail.

13.1 If Statement

In the 'if' statement we get the chance to perform an action only if a certain condition evaluates to true.

The general syntax of the 'if' statement is given below.

```
if(condition)
{
//Execute code
}
```

Example 53: The following program is used to showcase how to use the if statement.

```java
// This is a Java class
public class Demo
{
    // This is the main entry point of the Java program
    public static void main(String args[])
    {
        int i = 4;
        if (i < 5)
        {
        System.out.println("The value of i is less than 5");
        }
    }
}
```

Things to note about the above program:

- We are defining a condition in the 'if' statement which says that only if the value of 'i' is less than 5, should the program write to console the relevant string.

With this program, the output is as follows:

The value of i is less than 5

13.2 If-Else Statement

In the 'if-else' statement we have the option of executing an optional statement when the 'if' condition does not evaluate to true.

The general syntax of the 'if-else' statement is given below.

```
if(condition)
{
//Execute code
}
else
{
//Execute code
}
```

Example 54: The following program is used to showcase how to use the if-else statement.

```java
// This is a Java class
public class Demo
{
    // This is the main entry point of the Java program
    public static void main(String args[])
    {
        int i = 7;
        if (i < 5)
        {
            System.out.println("The value of i is less than 5");
        }
        else
        {
            System.out.println("The value of i is more than 5");
        }
    }
}
```

With this program, the output is as follows:

The value of i is more than 5

13.3 Switch Statement

The 'switch' statement helps us to evaluate multiple options at one time and then execute code based on those various options.

The general syntax of the 'switch' statement is given below.

```
switch(expression)
{
  case constant-expression :
    statement(s);
    break;

  case constant-expression :
    statement(s);
    break;

  default :
  statement(s);
}
```

In the 'switch' statement, you can evaluate the condition against multiple expressions. For each matching expression you can have a corresponding statement to execute. Once the statement is found, the break statement can help to exit from the switch statement. You can also have a default statement which gets executed if neither of the expressions matches the condition in the switch statement.

Example 55: The following program is used to showcase how to use the switch statement.

```java
// This is a Java class
public class Demo
{
    // This is the main entry point of the Java program
    public static void main(String args[])
    {
        int i=4;
        switch (i)
        {
            case 1: System.out.println("The value of i is 1");
                break;

            case 2: System.out.println("The value of i is 2");
                break;

            case 3: System.out.println("The value of i is 3");
                break;

            case 4: System.out.println("The value of i is 4");
                break;

            default: System.out.println("The value of i is unknown");
                break;
        }
    }
}
```

Things to note about the above program:

- We are defining the switch statement to evaluate the value of 'i'.

- We are defining the different possible values of 'i' using the case statements.

- We finally define the default statement, which gets executed if none of the case statements match the desired expression.

With this program, the output is as follows:

The value of i is 4

13.4 Nested Statements

We can also make use of nested statements in decision making. Let's look at some examples of nested statements.

Example 56: The following program shows how to use the nested decision making statements.

```java
// This is a Java class
public class Demo
{
    // This is the main entry point of the Java program
    public static void main(String args[])
    {
        int i=4;
        if (i > 0)
        {
            if (i == 4)
            {
                System.out.println("The value is 4");
            }
        }
    }
}
```

In the above program we are making use of multiple if statements in the program.

With this program, the output is as follows:

The value of i is 4

Let's look at another example of using nested decision making statements.

Example 57: The following program shows how to use the nested decision making statements.

```java
// This is a Java class
public class Demo
{
   // This is the main entry point of the Java program
   public static void main(String args[])
   {
     int i = 4;
     if (i > 0)
     {
       switch (i)
       {
         case 1:
           System.out.println("The value of i is 1");
           break;

         case 2:
           System.out.println("The value of i is 2");
           break;

         case 3:
           System.out.println("The value of i is 3");
           break;

         case 4:
```

```
            System.out.println("The value of i is 4");
            break;

        default:
            System.out.println("The value of i is unknown");
            break;
        }
      }
    }
}
```

With this program, the output is as follows:

The value of i is 4

Conclusion

You have made it to the end of the first book in our Step-By-Step Java series. If you enjoyed getting started with Java, there is so much more to learn and do with this wonderful language. Be sure to continue your journey with the second book in the series, which looks at slightly more complex topics while still being beginner friendly.

JAVA

A Detailed Approach to Practical Coding

a. FREE Kindle Version with Paperback

Java is a valuable programming language with a large array of uses. It is practical, efficient, and extremely easy to use. It will be a great asset and reference point for your future in programming. If you can think it, you can create it. Don't be afraid to try something new.

Good luck and happy programming!

About the Author

Nathan Clark is an expert programmer with nearly 20 years of experience in the software industry.

With a master's degree from MIT, he has worked for some of the leading software companies in the United States and built up extensive knowledge of software design and development.

Nathan and his wife, Sarah, started their own development firm in 2009 to be able to take on more challenging and creative projects. Today they assist high-caliber clients from all over the world.

Nathan enjoys sharing his programming knowledge through his book series, developing innovative software solutions for their clients and watching classic sci-fi movies in his free time.

Made in the USA
Columbia, SC
06 May 2020